How to ^{un}⌃Spoil Your Child
fast

How to ^{un}Spoil Your Child fast

Richard Bromfield, PhD

Basil Books

ISBN-13:   978-0-9797885-1-2
ISBN: 0-9797885-1-X

Printed and bound in the United States of America.

*To the many parents and children
who have taught me well*

Contents

Contents

Acknowledgments

Thank you to my wife Debbie for encouraging my writing, serving as first reader, accompanying me as we tripped our way through our own parenting and, above all, for suggesting that the cover be yellow. And special thanks to journalist Rochelle Sharpe for helping to make the book better. Thanks also go to Vally Sharpe of United Writers Press for giving the book a design befitting its message, and to editor Virginia McRae who, with the gentlest touch, gave my manuscript a needed polish.

"I swear, my dear, you'll spoil that child."
~Thomas Congreve, 1694

Introduction

Does any of this sound familiar?

Your child whines, demands, and complains endlessly. She screams at the mall, tantrums in the restaurant, and holds her breath at home until she turns blue or gets her way. She shows little gratitude for what you do, seems to take it all for granted, ever asking for more.

No matter how much you do, she notices only what you haven't done for her in the last few minutes or hours. At the slightest frustration, she takes you to task, perhaps angrily, to tell you how bad you are or that you don't love her. You do and do but she is loath to do anything in return, and leaves you to battle for an ounce of cooperation.

Your words or instructions are seldom enough to satisfy her. Your child pushes for repeated explaining, accuses you of being unfair, and like some pint-sized lawyer, argues her point until, unable to take it anymore, you surrender and buy one more toy, let one more bedtime go, abandon one more limit.

If you live with all or even some of this, your child may be spoiled. But I bet you didn't need me to tell you that. You've probably known it yourself for months, maybe years.

Your inability to do something about it, however, has not been due to a lack of love or caring. Nor would you say that you don't care.

Her spoiled behavior matters to you a lot, and not just because of the way it stresses and torments you.

As much as your child frustrates and wears you out, your concerns go far beyond what it's been like for you to live under your child's tyranny. You worry what her being spoiled means for her well-being, not just at home, but on the playground and at school. You fear for her future, knowing that spoiled children often grow into spoiled adults unable to assume and manage the restraints, hardship, and responsibilities of adulthood. You realize that overindulged children may be prone to anxiety, depression, and troubled relationships. And you recognize that spoiled children risk "inheriting" skin that's too thin and brittle to defend them against the arrows and insults that life will fling their way.

You, better than anyone, know what life at home has been like and you fear the discouraging fate of your spoiled—dare I say entitled—child. More than any social critic or child psychologist, you know what you've been doing and what has to be done. Unfortunately and for all sorts of reasons, you just haven't been able to follow through or do differently.

Know and be consoled, however: You are not alone. A colossal number of today's parents spoil their children, arguably a majority. Although most of these parents are not happy about that state of family affairs, they may be stuck in a quagmire they feel helpless to escape from. Some loving parents may even fear that it's too late to reverse the damage done.

But they're wrong. It's not too late.

Borrowing from my more than twenty-five years of working with children and their parents, this book will serve as your guide to successfully unspoiling your child. My book distills all that I've seen into a rather simple, straightforward, and doable plan that will allow you to learn from other parents' trial and error. You don't have to spend years inventing your own wheel.

As a parent of college-aged children, I remember vividly the absolute exhaustion, confusion, frustration, and so on that came before. The parents of young children who I know are overworked and over-extended. The single mothers who I know are even more overworked and overextended. The parents who most need this book and the help it can offer have the least time, energy, and attention to read books about parenting or anything else. And so I strove to write a book that presents what's important in words and format that go down fast and easy.

And how should you use the book? Read it and apply it, going slowly, sticking with each new step until you see it take hold. Until new ideas and steps make sense to you and feel more natural. Until they work for you and your child. For most garden varieties of spoiled children, this method will work as fast as you want it to, meaning as fast as you are game to apply it. As a bonus, my approach can also benefit many children who have greater troubles and who now go by assorted names such as impulsive, distractible, disorganized, bipolar, difficult, and oppositional.

Run with this book and, before you know it, things will look up. Before you know it, both you and your child will change in ways you never imagined possible.

RB

Parents Have Rights, Too

As a good parent, you deserve:

- ❖ a position of authority and respect
- ❖ appreciation for what you do
- ❖ private times and places that exclude your child
- ❖ to dote on, not just your child, but also on your spouse, partner, and self
- ❖ to trust your own judgment concerning parenting matters
- ❖ to pursue interests beyond your child
- ❖ to consider what you yourself want, too, when making family and personal decisions

❖ forgiveness, your own and theirs, for
your inevitable moments of moodiness,
impatience, and other human conditions
often judged to be the exclusive province
of children

Not demanding these rights can harm you and
your child.

Note to Readers

To avoid the tedium of he and she, her or him, or worse, the awkwardness of s/he, I have tried to randomly refer to both girls and boys. Girls and boys can be equally spoiled, of course, and neither gender is any easier or harder to unspoil than the other.

Also, you will notice that I seldom refer to a child's age. This is deliberate. Though what I say mostly applies to young children, much of it bears relevance to older kids and teens, too. I will leave it to you to customize the methods to your own child. After all, who knows your child better?

1

Reality Check

We have a problem. Or, more to the point, you have a problem. Or do you? I ask because I've learned the hard and slow way not to assume too much. Listen to this true story about a mother whom I'll call Sadie, and you'll understand what I mean. Sadie had brought her seven-year-old son to therapy because his school had told her to.

"Sean, I guess, can get kind of a little demanding sometimes," Sadie began. She settled back into the big blue chair across from my own and picked at a thread on the chair's worn arm. Her son smiled at me from the corner, where he sat on the floor building a small LEGO boat.

Sadie was an intelligent, educated, and articulate woman. I couldn't help noticing her choice of words. *I guess, kind of, a little,* and *sometimes,* words that couldn't have been more tentative and less committed.

"At least that's what his teacher says," Sadie added.

"*At least that's what his teacher says*," Sean mouthed silently, while he mocked his mother's look of concern.

Sadie, Sean, and I had been meeting for thirty minutes. The office looked as if several children had played there for hours. Sheets of paper with hastily drawn airplanes covered the desk and floor. A long, curving domino knockdown lay fallen across one end of the room. Twisted pipe cleaners and assorted toys lay strewn about the containers they'd been taken from. There were crumbs and a juice stain on the rug, remnants of Sean's snack. "We were so busy playing video games this morning that we didn't have time to eat breakfast," Sadie explained while she rushed to pick up the half-eaten granola bar that Sean had tossed aside.

Sadie's use of the royal we was not lost on me. And it wasn't that she hadn't tried to get her only son to clean up after himself. I'd heard her ask him over and over. She'd asked sweetly and quietly, coaxing but gentle, begging and embarrassed, her irritation and impotence growing louder and clearer. I wondered to myself how many times that morning she'd called Sean to breakfast. Once, twice, thirteen times? But that was then and this was now.

"You say that Sean's teachers think he can be bossy," I went on. "What do you think?"

Sean stopped playing and studied his mother's reaction to my question.

"Sean can be a very good boy," Sadie replied. "He can be very helpful and cooperative when he wants to."

"Does he want to very often?" I asked. Sean chuckled and went back to playing with the blocks.

Sadie reached into the oversized satchel at her feet. "I brought a yogurt, too. Do you want that? Oh, and there's a bag of chips." "Any pretzels?" Sean snapped.

"No, just yogurt—"

"I told you to bring pretzels!"

Sadie turned red. "I know, I know," she said to me. You're thinking he's the boss. And I don't blame you. It must look awful, as if I just wait on him and never say no." I smiled. There was nothing more for me to say. She was saying it all.

"I don't want you to think I'm making excuses. But we really did have a crazy weekend with a house full of guests. None of us got much sleep. And we ate horribly. It was my fault. Sean ate way too much sugar."

In my clinical experience, parents commonly credit their children's misbehavior to candy, soda, late nights, and early mornings. The excitement of vacations and the stress of school. Fatigue and illness, allergies and rainy days. Full moons, and because it's Thursday. Sadie's excuses might have struck me as humorous had she not so wanted to believe them.

It was near the hour's end, and Sadie once more asked Sean to clean up the mess he'd made. Sean kicked off his sneaker. Sadie asked Sean to get his shoe even as she walked over to pick it up herself. Seizing the moment, Sean jumped up and stole her seat. Sadie looked at the big chair, then backed up a few steps and sat in a smaller, less comfortable, and less central seat near my desk.

"But wasn't that your chair?" I asked.

"This chair is fine, really." Smug in his triumph, Sean buried himself deep into his mother's chair.

I could have persisted. But what would I have accomplished? Probably little more than humiliating a mother who was feeling extremely inadequate. Years ago I'd witnessed the sad scene of a mother trying to wrestle her chair back from her child. Once was plenty.

"Is it always like this?" I asked gently.

Sadie's eyes teared. She nodded. "I don't know where it went wrong." She spoke softly. "I never wanted it to get like this." "Are we going to McDonald's? Sean asked, oblivious to his mother's upset. "I'm hungry."

This is not fiction. It happened. In fact, hours resembling that one happen a lot. In my office and more so in countless homes with countless families who will never set eyes on a therapist.

Twenty-four/seven, or whatever remains after school and sleep, millions of mothers and fathers are beset by bossy and demanding children. Day after day, these parents put up with—did someone say, invite?—unrelenting and unreasonable requests that they, the parents, go out of their way to fulfill, often blindly and without question. It took Sadie many months of weekly therapy to open her eyes wide enough to see her situation clearly and to begin restoring proper and healthy balance to her home.

How about you? Are you ready to open your eyes?

2

Where to Start?

Fixing up an old house is an intricate business. You need to identify all of the problems and proceed in some order that makes sense. You do the plumbing and electrical work behind the walls before you paint and wallpaper them. You sand and revarnish wood floors after you install and plaster new ceilings. The sequence in which you rebuild a house matters. Fortunately, this is not so true when it comes to renovating your parenting.

Pick a card, any card. In a sea of indulgence and misbehavior, where does a parent begin? Practically speaking, anywhere. Pursuit of the perfect point of entry is a roadblock that serves mostly to avoid the task of unspoiling your child.

It's obvious why we procrastinate distasteful jobs like doing our taxes or cleaning the attic.

Parents just as frequently put off parenting that will force them to behave in new ways and to reckon not just with their child, but with themselves.

Make it simple. Slaying a gigantic, three-headed serpent is a labor worthy of Hercules. Solving Fermat's Last Theorem and unraveling the genetic code are best left to keener intellects than ours. (Though take it from me as gospel, Nobel Prize–winning scientists have the same parenting issues that we do.)

I urge parents to pick an easier first task, something they can succeed at. Aim for a single, one-act play that will convey potency and intent, that will say loud and clear: It's a new day and things are going to change around here!

Psyche yourself. You are about to do battle. Prepare yourself for the new regime you are about to unleash. "It's long overdue," remind yourself. "It is needed." "I am doing this for my child's sake." "I am being brave." "I am being responsible." "I am being a parent." "I am being Parent."

Know, too, that it's not only okay, it's good to regularly update your parenting and the rules of the home. Just because you may have been a bit lax for some months or years doesn't mean you can't get tougher. It takes a wise leader to look in the mirror and see when change is called for.

Hold on tight. I know, this sounds pathetically dramatic. Are you about to ride Niagara Falls in a barrel or race Motocross? Not exactly. You are probably in no physical danger. You will, though, be at risk of falling off your steed as you approach the gates of the castle you're storming.

Okay, I'm making this worse. What I'm trying to say is that you may lose your gumption as you go head-to-head—or more like midriff-to-head—with that thirty-six-inch child of yours.

By the way, how did such a little thing grow so powerful?

3

The Signs of a Spoiling Parent

Parents go through much, if not all, of their family day with their eyes glued to the road. Getting through a day is taxing enough. Who has the energy and interest to look back to see what transpired?

Take a moment and see how many of these spoiling symptoms apply to you and your parenting:

- ❖ Your child doesn't listen to you
- ❖ Your child mistreats you
- ❖ You make excuses for your child's behavior
- ❖ You rescue your child from consequences
- ❖ You do your child's chores or homework
- ❖ You yell a lot
- ❖ You feel like a nag
- ❖ You say mean things to your child

❖ You find yourself bargaining and promising rewards for every bit of cooperation

❖ You repeatedly threaten, warn, and count to three

❖ You seldom follow through

❖ You let things slide and slide until you explode

❖ You explain, over and over, everything you ask of your child

❖ You seldom, if ever, say no

❖ You walk on eggshells lest you upset or displease your child

❖ Much of the time parenting feels like you're driving an out-of-control race car

❖ You have too many moments, lasting days or weeks or longer, when you do not like your child or when you wonder why you became a parent*

---

*These signs were first listed in the book *How to Turn Boys into Men Without a Man Around the House: A Single Mother's Guide* that I cowrote with family therapist Cheryl Erwin (Random House, 2001).

A child needs boundaries and structure to grow and will seek them when they are absent. A child who perpetually pesters her parent may be searching for the limits she needs to grow straight. Her demanding and disruptive behavior is meant, to a great degree, to test you, her parent, to find out what outrageous action will finally get you to react—constructively.

That deep down inside your child wants firmer parenting is nearly always proven by the calmer, more cooperative, and more contented child you discover in the hours or days following a stuck-to act of unspoiling.

4

Grab Their Attention

Parents need to make a firm decision in their own heads. They need to hold a referendum on their parenting and vote to override the status quo. They need to send a clear message to themselves that they choose to improve their parenting. Parents need to commit to their vision of a happier and more contented home as if it's as grave a mandate as better schools or world peace.

"But don't we have to announce our intentions?" parents ask. "Don't we need to give the kids fair warning?"

"Let's see," I replied to one parent who was tired of asking her son to brush his teeth. "He's now eleven years old, which means you've given him...twelve (per day) x 365 (days per year) x eight (years)...more than 35,000 warnings. That's about

34,950 more warnings than he deserved and needed."
Not to mention he was a bright boy with enough memory to remember 493 species of Pokémon.

And he needs one more reminder?

No. Although writing a Proclamation of Unspoiling might be a worthwhile exercise for yourself, there's no need to show or read it to your child. Nor do you need to stand on a milk crate and declare to the family your war on childhood indulgence and entitlement. Haven't loud voices and verbal threats proven their futility by now?

To paraphrase one great president, "Talk softly and carry a big shtick." By shtick, I mean a real good trick up your sleeve, a big deed that, better than any speech or threat, will show your child you mean it, that the party's over.

As a good example, consider Kelsey. Kelsey's mom, a lovely woman and good parent, came to me because her son had become a brute. Napoleon who?

As far as she knew, she lived with the original Little Emperor. In laying out just how spoiled he was, she admitted that for months she'd been taking Kelsey to the toy store immediately after his weekly therapy session. "I didn't know any other way to get him here."

We came up with a plan. A plan that both intrigued and frightened Kelsey's mother. It went like this: She'd leave after Kelsey's next hour as if nothing was different. She'd take him to the toy store and buy him his expected reward for having seen me. She'd leave the toy store and head off to run her own errands, just as she'd always done. But when Kelsey would yell that he was not going with her and demand that she drive him home that very minute—*Get this!*—instead of driving home, she'd turn her car around and drive right back to the toy store. She'd calmly take Kelsey's toy and bag and walk back in. She'd refrain from yelling or threatening or saying anything as to what she was doing or why.

"His jaw dropped. He couldn't believe it," Kelsey's mother told me that night by phone. She described how he'd kept yelling at her, "You can't do this! It's against the law!"

What had she done? Nothing more and nothing less than quietly walking back into the store and returning the toy she'd just bought.

Kelsey's mother felt especially proud that, when asked if there was a problem with the toy, she candidly replied that her son had been quite rude and so she wished to bring it back.

The message was not wasted on Kelsey. He saw in living color and in one fell swoop that his mother had changed. She'd thrown out of whack all his expectations and assumptions as to what his mother would tolerate and what she would never do. Though his mother had to go through this routine a few more times, she considered it a mere refresher course for a life lesson whose first impressions had struck the deepest and hardest.

She just as well could have returned things that parents seldom think about taking away. Things like sports equipment and back to school supplies and clothes. Or, she could have targeted a different behavior with her grand gesture.

Is tooth-brushing a problem for your child? Try no treats for the entire next day. No warnings, no threats, just a total prohibition of sugar and sweets for the following twenty-four hours. Is he repeatedly late for school? Try to stop nagging him to go. Instead, consider letting him deal with the consequences of his constant tardiness. No more need for your anger or your making excuses for him.* Does he refuse to clean up his toys? Put them all away for a few days, period. Is he rude after you give him something nice, like a treat or his allowance? Snatch it right back.

As you'll soon see in more detail, other smashing openings might involve leaving restaurants with food on the table or walking out in the middle of a movie.

---

*This can work effectively for all but the truly school phobic or resistant child, in which case you might have a bigger issue than spoiling.

5

What's Wrong with Spoiled Anyway?

Parents, teachers, spiritual leaders, pediatricians, child psychologists, and even grandparents agree on one thing: Children need love and discipline. And children need to learn life skills to thrive. They need to learn to wait, to work hard and cope with failure, to admit and correct errors, to realize and make amends for misdeeds, and so on. Most parents could come up with their own lists.

But many of these same parents have neglected the principles of parenting they themselves hold true and dear. Whether determined for good reason not to parent anything like their stricter mothers and fathers, or believing that esteem-stroking makes for happier children, or just too plain weary or unmotivated to do otherwise, the outcome has been the same. Too often parents give in to their whining, demanding, discontented, and misbehaving children. We all know the immediate cost of our leniency: the crying, the fussing, the noise, and the fighting. But what is the greater price our children pay for our lax parenting?

Good character and psychological health don't just happen. Nor is love by itself enough. Without proper discipline children go forward on shaky ground. When children self-govern, when they live by the royal me, they grow into tortured adults, along the way torturing everyone else with their ill-boding I's: *Inconsiderate, Irritable, Irresponsible, Impulsive, Immature, Insatiable,* and if severe enough, *Immoral.* These indulged children may further deceive themselves with *Illusions* of grandeur and *Invincibility.*

Deprived of sufficient constancy and dependable limits, structure, and expectations, not knowing where they themselves end and others begin, they fail to learn tolerance for the many experiences of life that are less than exciting or instantly rewarding, and that involve stress, failure, and hard work. As a result, indulged kids can grow into chronic underachievers who cannot sustain interest and effort in their learning, work, and connections with people. Children who forever disrupt home life can wholly ruin a peaceful house to the point where parents lose sight of what they liked about being parents. Children who disrupt their classrooms can likewise push away teachers.

At its most extreme, overindulgence can make children prone to delinquency, substance abuse, sexual mishap, and troubled relationships. And not so obviously, spoiling can lead quieter and more compliant children to experience unnecessary anxiety, withdrawal, and problems with anger.

By trying to make life too easy, by striving to bring only smiles and laughter, parents actually risk creating precisely what they fear most: children with paper-thin esteem who haplessly rely on the outside and things for stimulation, satisfaction, happiness, and, most sadly, purpose. At the end of the day, whatever the issues in their home, it is often the parents who feel they have failed their children. And there are few feelings more painful for a parent to know.

One last warning. Don't blame your child for being spoiled. When overly frustrated, irritated, or disheartened, parents are prone to strike out. "You're selfish." "You're a brat!" "I don't know how you got so spoiled." On the contrary, you know only too well.*

*Much of this discussion was adapted or borrowed from that same book on single mothers and sons.

6

More Than Meets the Eye

I have now worked with many parents who've marched their spoiled sons and daughters back to the mall or who have performed equivalent grand gestures. Why does such a simple act work? What wields its power? Is it magic or a scam?

My observations, insights, and strategies, however handy and simplistic, are based on an understanding of children that runs deep and is subtle and complex. What Kelsey's mom did might have looked like glib schtick, but it was a deliberate and well-founded act based on child development. It's worth our delving into its underlying mechanics.

Kelsey's mother could have said things like: "From now on, I'm not going to spoil you." "Starting next week I'm not buying you any more toys just for going to therapy." "You're going to run my errands whether you like it or not." "You have to give me the consideration I deserve, just like I give you." Not that any of those would have been harmful or untrue. They just would have been feeble and would have sounded, to her son, like more mealy mush to be brushed off his sleeve.

Instead of another idle threat, Kelsey's mom delivered the hard goods that hit him where it hurt. She let her action and its consequences do the talking, all of which defied the laws driving their shared universe.

You can't do this! But I just did, her steady and quiet actions stated clearly.

You can't return things you already bought me. But I just did.

You can't betray me like that, telling a strange clerk that I am rude. But I did.

You can't renege on your (unspoken) promise to bribe me every week. Ditto, goes the chorus.

You owe me, big time. True, absolutely true. I owe you to be the best parent I can be, even when it's hard and potentially embarrassing for me.

What just happened? In one swift power move Kelsey's mother turned her son's world on its ears, and warned him what was coming more clearly than anything printed in a *New York Times* headline or announced over the speakers at Fenway Park.

Because her action spoke loudest, Kelsey's mother could save her voice and heart for more important matters. She didn't need to scream at her son as she always had. She didn't need to tell him how selfish, inconsiderate, or bad he was. Nor did she need to explain why she'd done what she did. He knew why, and in case he didn't, he'd heard what she'd said to the toy store clerk.

But as his mother would have been happy to tell you, he tried like mad to blame her. "You stink." "You're a terrible mother." "I hate you." "You lie." "You're mean." "You don't love me." And maybe the toughest for a parent to hear, "I don't love you."

I reminded her that the desperation of Kelsey's tirade attested to its futility. "Kelsey knows the score. He knows who truly is to blame."

Which brings us to the remaining beauty of what happened. Not only did Kelsey learn the undesired consequences of his rudeness (losing the toy), he also had to face the awful truth. It was his own fault. It was Kelsey who now sat with the empty toy bag that said it all.

Kelsey's mother didn't have to punish the anger and frustration and self-disappointment that came in the hours afterward. Her son could rant and rave all he wanted. Kelsey promised to do better and begged for another chance to go back to the toy store that afternoon. "I'll run your errands with you," he pleaded. "I'll say thank you and be helpful." But his mother had no need to take his bait. She knew he'd have umpteen chances to make it right and better, tomorrow and probably every day of his childhood. But it wouldn't happen now. For today, his bag would remain empty.

Kelsey was distraught. But his mother could take it. Nothing could make her back down. Nothing could make her undo the huge splash she'd made.

And last, because her calm and responsible deed had addressed her growing frustration and caught her son's attention, she had no need to stay angry with him. In fact, having set the consequence and then hanging tough, she felt free to feel for her son's predicament.

"I know how disappointed you are," she told him. "I know that pretty soon you're going to make better choices." Though Kelsey pushed her empathy and hugs away, he knew she felt bad that he had to go through this, just as he felt loved because she'd cared enough to take the parenting road less easy.

7

It Can Be Done

Spoil is a funny word. We suppose that most of us grasp its meaning pretty well in the jargon of family life. We let the kids have ice cream without eating their dinners. We let them stay up too late. We buy them gifts too often or even after they've behaved badly. Or we buys gifts that cost too much. We coddle, we pamper.

When I look up "spoil" in my old and beat-up *Webster's Collegiate Dictionary*, I find the definition that we're looking for:

> "to impair [a child's] disposition or character by overindulgence or excessive praise."

Parents' relationship to that word—spoil—is complex and at first blush seems contradictory. On the one hand we routinely and unthinkingly indulge our children with as much thought as we use grabbing milk from the fridge. And yet, when something in life jolts us and makes us take notice that our children are spoiled, our parenting minds short-circuit and spark to the opposite pole. In those rarer and disquieting moments, rather than dismiss and minimize, parents declare a graver sentence, as if their spoiled children are as ruined as rotten bananas.

When it comes to the greatest number of children and families, however, most spoiled children can be fixed, changed, and unspoiled. But what does it take to accomplish that? Consider the determination and commitment that one couple showed me.

Leni and Karl sought my help for their eight-year-old daughter, Stephanie, who suffered great anxiety. They asked to first meet with me without their daughter, so that they might discuss their concerns openly. They described a home life that, they felt, was "rapidly imploding." Together they told how Stephanie would cry and scream when going to school.

"We've worked out this crazy arrangement," Karl explained. "We both drive our cars to the school. I say my good-bye and then—"

"A real big good-bye," Leni interrupted.

Karl nodded in agreement. "Then Leni walks Stephanie to her classroom until her teacher takes over and she quiets down."

"Does that work well?" I asked.

Stephanie's parents looked at each other and laughed.

"Not really," Leni replied. "It seems almost to make things worse. The teacher says we should back off, that Steph does fine once we leave. She even suggested we let someone else take Steph to school. Believe it or not, I could handle it. But Steph would never go for it." Her husband nodded.

"And we can't go anywhere anymore," Leni continued, her tone more sad than complaining.

"It's as if our world is closing in on us." They told about the horrific tantrums that Stephanie threw when they'd tried going to dinner or a movie without her. On two occasions—when they'd decided for their daughter's sake that they just had to force themselves to go out—a flurry of panicked cell phone calls from Stephanie and the babysitter made short work of their night out. Bedtimes were no better. Stephanie stayed up as late as she wished. "She controls everything in the house," Karl said. "We need help. All three of us. We just want our home back, and we don't care what it takes or how long or what it costs." But those words were spoken in the first meeting, when parents feel desperate.

In our second meeting, Stephanie's parents raised a new and different agenda. While they wanted their daughter to get whatever treatment she needed, they sought "to get this thing over as quickly as possible." They made clear that they had plenty of other appointments and activities to occupy their schedules just as they had better ways to spend their money. "Tell us what to do," Karl said, "and we'll do it."

I sighed. No offense taken. But how many times before had I heard parents pledge to change overnight. And why wouldn't they? Why shouldn't parents want their children to get better fast and with minimal pain, cost, and effort? Of course, parents would vow to change their ways—even if they wouldn't, even if they couldn't. And yet, I soon learned something new and different from these parents.

With extraordinary candor, Leni and Karl spent the remainder of that second hour coming clean. They told me of having indulged Stephanie not just lately but over her lifetime. Instead of blaming each other, each confessed his and her own litany of parenting crimes, as if eagerly competing for Worst Parent of the Year. Their motivation seemed genuine and so I offered them a challenge. "Try sending her to school tomorrow with a friend."

The next morning Leni called me to say that Stephanie had gone to school with a neighbor, and that it had gone fine, once she'd gotten into the car, that is. Leni admitted that it had been hard, and that she'd come close to giving up during the frenzy. Buoyed, Leni and Karl took Stephanie's and their own success that day and leveraged it toward a second parenting challenge. Rather than rest on their laurels, each step ahead energized their taking the next.

Within days Stephanie's parents were seeing a happier and calmer child. They'd also begun to discover in themselves the parents they'd always wanted to be. They'd stopped and reversed the vicious cycle so that it now spun healthily upward.

At the end of the day, or in about six weeks, they'd triumphed.

As a clinician who has been seeing families for twenty-seven years now, I could have told a gloomier and more common story about a family that took much longer or wholly failed to get their homes back in order. But you already know about shortcomings and procrastination. I preferred to share an instance where things went well, relatively smoothly, and rather quickly. It can work.

Were Leni and Karl überparents who could do what no one else can?

Not at all. They were average in most every way. Except for their motivation. Much like you, they loved their child, were tired of the battles, and did not want to spend time and money on therapists. What distinguished Stephanie's parents was how they supercharged their ordinary motivation to an intensity where they couldn't just ignore, deny, or step over it one more second.

8

The Buck Stops Where?

The beauty of a startlingly novel intervention—like going back to a store and returning something that you'd bought your child—resides in its simplicity and clarity. You know exactly why you are doing it, and so does your child. You live out a three-dimensional picture that speaks much more than a thousand words ever could. That your child "hears" your actions in a way that she'd never listen to your thousand words is just a bonus. For many averagely spoiled children, a crackling first step such as the one taken by Kelsey's mother will wake your child and get the unspoiling ball rolling.

Without a big kick-off, it may be hard to get your child's attention. Some parents walk on eggshells out of a realization that they have no reliable limit they can rely on. Rather than confront

49

that frightening, if common reality, parents dance around it, forever talking and negotiating with their child, deceiving themselves that they're in control, seldom getting the behavior and reaction they want. Kind of like, when you really want to tell your misbehaving child that there will be no ice cream tonight, yet sensing your powerlessness, you tell her in the firmest voice you can muster, "Okay, that's it. Your choice is chocolate or vanilla. If you don't pick one, I'm going to choose for you." *Ouch. I may only get my second favorite flavor.*

If you think I'm kidding, and it doesn't show up in your own parenting, just check out what's going on around you the next time you're in line at the local Ben & Jerry's.

In order to establish any kind of authoritative parenting—and by authoritative, I mean parenting that is all at once firm, nurturing, fair, judicious, prudent, confident…you get the picture—there has to be some place where you can dependably draw a line in the sand that your child will not cross. Far too many parents do not dare put a stone on their shoulder for they know without question that their child will knock it off. Is there anything more disheartening and dismaying to watch than a full-sized adult backing down for a half-sized toddler? And why is it that we cannot seem to see when it's happening to us, when we are the ones grown lily-livered?

What are the implications for parenting without a secure endpoint? Ask a teacher who's seen detentions lose their meaning for a student. I've worked with wayward teens whose misbehavior has earned them detentions that they skip, and which leads to more detentions that reproduce like bunnies.

"How are they going to make me go to fifty-four detentions?" laughed one adolescent. "There's only three weeks of school left."

Parenting under such peril is like walking a tightrope. But not the circus kind that runs over a safety net. I mean the kind that's jury-rigged between skyscrapers across Seventh Avenue. A few millimeters to the right or left and it's splat time in Gotham City. Of course, I speak metaphorically. Parents don't really get flattened. Instead, their children just go through life at the mercy of their wishes and impulses, everyone's agreed-upon recipe for disaster.

If you are a parent in such misfortune, you have even greater reason to implement a big first step. Take a gulp, a deep breath, maybe say a Hail Mary, and rub a rabbit's foot or two. You and your child can't afford to lose another day. Though your work will be tough and the storm you unleash mighty, keep in mind, that is the price parents pay for having let things go.

Your child may be of the variety that pushes you harder, and closer to the brink. She may throw a tantrum that registers on the Richter scale. She may turn red with rage or blue from holding her breath. She may throw things, break things, and say things. But for all of its heat and blowing, it's only wind and bluff. (Except when it's a foot through the wall. Then it's only sheet-rock, which you will have her help to fix.)

Do just as Kelsey's mother did and hold steady. While the tumult you experience will likely outdo Kelsey's, your outcome can be as constructive and as hopeful. Give in, however, and you may eventually find yourself in thicker quicksand with children who are bigger, badder, and more resistant to renewal.*

* If your child grows very aggressive or violent, or if you are losing control, professional help might be called for.

9

Just Do It

When you think about it, loving your kids to death is an odd expression. But we parents know just what it means. Sometimes the love we feel for our children is more than words can capture, more than we can bear. Summer knew that feeling well.

Summer adored her children. Divorced from a neglectful and abusive man, the children's father, she wanted nothing more than to make their lives good. Not wanting her children to be the products of a broken home, she'd stayed with that man too long. There was nothing Summer would not do for her children. It made no difference how tired or ill she felt, or whether she had her own work to do, her children's needs came first.

"I know. I know. I know," Summer would say to me when she and her children would walk into my waiting room, always carrying bags of candy, bakery goods, and toys. She was the kind of mother who rose early to make pancakes shaped like hearts and who often put surprises in the children's lunch boxes. She'd buy them birthday and Christmas gifts that outran her budget. "I couldn't get them a good father," she said. "The least I can do is give them all that I can give them." It wasn't until her debt got out of hand that Summer was forced to change her ways.

It'd be an easy shot to criticize Summer. It doesn't take Sigmund Freud to figure out that no amount of goodies and toys will make up for a split family. But then again, who of us doesn't know that impulse, the wish to distract our children or give them something to make them smile, that will for the moment make them forgot what we know or imagine to be their misery?

Many other parents, especially those in my own boomer generation, indulge their children in direct reaction to the childhoods and parenting they knew. Many parents have told me that they love to say yes because when they were children all they heard was no. These parents indulge and give—things, attention, and affection—less out of unconscious resentment and more out of a conscious choice to nourish their children's joy and spirit. They wish to foster in their children the capacities to want, ask, take, and enjoy from life in a way that they, the parents, never could. It's not rare to meet parents who can indulge and spend on their children in a way they would never do for themselves.

My many years of working with parents tell me there are many other good reasons why parents spoil their children. These reasons are as varied as the faces of children and can include:

- ❖ fatigue
- ❖ uncertainty as to what to do
- ❖ fear of angering your child
- ❖ fear of hurting your child
- ❖ fear of not being your child's best friend
- ❖ fear that your child won't like you
- ❖ rebellion against your own parents
- ❖ preoccupation with work or other things
- ❖ fear that you'll undo their esteem
- ❖ distraction by marital strife

- ❖ worn down by single parenting
- ❖ unwilling to make the time or effort
- ❖ guilt
- ❖ (unconscious) pleasure in your child's misbehavior or defying

Unfortunately, you and your child cannot afford to wait for insights into your reasons, reasons that often run deep and far outside your awareness. You can try psychoanalysis to uncover those reasons. By the time you get off the couch, unfortunately, your child will be grown up and gone. Your child needs an adjustment that begins reasonably soon, like yesterday.

By now, you have been making changes and have been seeing some signs of improvement. Hold and cherish these first steps as proof that you are on the right track. As your unspoiling grows more effective, you will find that it generalizes to other aspects of your parenting. As you continue to gain experience, for example, in your ability to discipline, your child will need less of it.

You should also find that as your parenting and child improve, so will your understanding of what deterred you from doing it earlier, leading to yet better and easier parenting. As is true for your golf and tennis swing, the more efficient the technique, the less effort and attention you'll exert. Though much of parenting isn't second nature, parents can learn those skills until they become more natural and reflexive.

As you will soon discover, if you haven't already, unrelenting forces will work to undermine your efforts to unspoil. Like gremlins throwing wrenches into the works, these forces will tenaciously toil to weaken your resolve and sabotage your strategies. Your guilt may goad you to give in and give up. But you won't. Instead, you will grab that guilt by the horns and channel it into preventing a different regret: not giving your children the parenting they need, not preparing them for life.

It is human for parents to rationalize that their children are young and that they'll outgrow their spoiling, or that there'll be plenty of time to unspoil them when they're older. Financial planners tell us that contributing in early years to our IRAs is worth more than contributing for the following twenty-five years. So it is with children. The earlier you unspoil them, the better.

10

Law and Order

You've got your child's attention. You've declared war on spoiling and appear to have won the first encounter. At least for a few hours, your child knew you meant business, and now she probably wonders whether you've got the stamina and stomach to keep going. Although she won't curl up and give in, she's curious and a little apprehensive. That effective first step was a wake-up call. You now have a whole "day" of unspoiling to plan and implement. Where to next?

Before we invent a second and specific strategy, we need to reexamine the ladder of power in your home. I assume there is some question as to who's in control. And this book, with its methods, intends to put you back in charge where you belong.

And before you can win that big competition, you might need to level the playing field or maybe even tilt it in your favor. As we'll see together, there are many ways to do this. The foremost requisite, though, is that you immediately adjourn the court. What do I mean?

Today's parents, and I'm no exception, tend to talk with their kids. In many ways that is a good change from previous generations. There are many children who will discuss their dearest experiences and concerns with their parents openly and with trust. How can that not be a blessing? But I'm not here to celebrate parent-child conversation. My mission is to help you unspoil your child.

Today's parents also tend to be less comfortable with their authority. Instead of telling their child what to do, they ask. Demands become questions, questions turn into special elections. When my children were young, I was just as guilty of this as the next parent, and yet my eyes roll when I overhear other parents doing the same thing.

Look what "Please hand me that stick" can morph into at the playground.

"Sweetie, may mommy have that stick?"

"Would you like to give mommy that stick?"

"Wouldn't you rather play with this shovel than that nasty old stick?" *No, no and still no, says the child's behavior.*

"Can you pretty please give mommy the stick, and then we'll go to the candy store?" *Now we're getting somewhere.*

"That's a good girl. Wait, wait, come back and give me the stick now or we're not going to go to the candy store." *I want a better deal.*

"If you don't bring it right now, you're only getting one thing at the candy store." *You mean one thing or one bag?*

"You're only going to get one bag of one kind of candy." *But I want a whistle pop, too.*

"Then you'd better come give me the stick right this second." *And a gummy snake?*

"Yes!" mother says, "and a gummy snake. What a good girl you are!" *That's more like it.*

You get the point. Just as you can understand how, over time, a parent comes to feel resentment, frustration, and impotence. "Damn it! Give me that stick before I..." *Gee*, the child is left to wonder, *why didn't you just say you wanted it in the first place?*

We don't just say so because...I'm actually not quite sure why. But we don't. And that is a major problem for you and your child.

So what's my point besides embarrassing the two of us? It's time to disbar your mini-attorney.

From this page on, you will no longer offer up twenty-six reasons why you want your daughter to clean her room. Nor will you explain and reexplain why you want the Game Cube shut off.

Children argue their points with their parents much in the ways that major corporations do. Both parties seek to delay what seem like inevitable decisions and penalties. As long as your child questions, debates, and opposes bedtime, she guarantees that she stays up. The battle itself is gratifying. As long as the two of you (verbally) lock horns, you are engaged in a tangle that looks something like a tango.

The analogy to a civil lawsuit bears greater relevance. Sue a wrongful party and they will do everything to draw it out. They'll stop at nothing that might sap your strength, consume your resources, and undermine your resolve.

How long will they go at you? Until the fifty-ninth minute of the twenty-third hour and then some. They know from experience that they can wear people down. Their aim and hope? That you will tire and fade, and give up the case or settle. For a guilty company, a settlement represents a victory that allows it to save both face and money.

Your child likewise has little to lose by battling you to the end. If she loses, she has to go to bed, brush her teeth, or clean up her toys. Hey, wait a minute, wasn't that the worst that could happen to her anyway? And what do you risk by allowing her to wrangle with you? Just about everything—sleep, a headache, self-respect, self-esteem, and so on. And what do you get if you win in the end? Nothing more than if you had been able to stick to your rightful case from the get-go.

Every time you do legal battle with your child, you empower her willingness to battle on and again. She gets stronger and better at it. Her taste and skill for negotiating sharpen. And, scariest of all, should you surrender in the final moments after a long trial, she will learn a treacherous lesson (treacherous for you, that is). She'll learn to never let up when dealing with you. For she's seen that, in the end, her persistence will do you in and she will triumph.

What can you do when your daughter interrogates you? *Refuse to play by her rules.* Who made her judge and jury? *Don't answer her questions.* Don't explain and explain yourself. Don't justify your parenting to her. Maybe even—I can't believe I'm saying this—tell her, "Because I am the parent and I said so."

Think of it. You're an educated adult who's had sex, backed into a tree, and lost money on lottery tickets. She hasn't even finished kindergarten. What does she know?

Case closed.

11

Who's Boss?

Anyone, including an entire village, can raise a good child. But it takes something special, an extra effort, to ruin a boy or girl. But it's done every day by parents just like you and me, people who never thought it possible. Can you do it, too? Answer yourself a resounding yes!

I know, you see others ruining their children, but the only child you really care about is your own. Of course, you can't help wondering how you can best go about ruining your own child.

What, your plaintive eyes ask me, is the surest and quickest route to achieving that goal?

Make your child head of the household. There is nothing like the smell and feel of raw power to undermine a child's growing sense of security and identity. Some parents lean toward the business model. They give their child the jobs of CEO, CFO, and COO. Some liberal parents elect their child to be President or Prime Minister. Other moms and dads are old-fashioned. They crown their daughter the Little Queen Mother or Empress. Whatever the preference, the result is the same—a child acquires power better suited to an older person, someone like a mother or a father.

But power is more than just a label. The child must be made to feel the specialness of her title. How can a parent do that? The surest route is to pretend, maybe even to believe, that your sole purpose in this world is to serve your child. (I do not mean nurturing and fulfilling her needs, as good parents should do that.) I mean her other needs— the ones that sound more like wishes, whimsy, and demands, needs that must override your own and every other family member's.

The golden rules? Never, ever allow your child to wait more than a few seconds for anything. (She's a Queen and has no need to learn to be patient.) You should have picked her up by the time her raised hands were fully vertical. While running to get her more juice is a good start, you should have headed for the kitchen before her glass ran empty. If she asks you a question, answer her instantly, even if it means ignoring your spouse. If you can anticipate what she will want without her having to ask, even better. Such a child should save her energy for more important duties, such as berating you when you fail to obey her quickly.

Much of the time your miniature monarch will handle her reign gracefully. With aplomb and delight she'll eagerly demand the goodies that should be brought for her pleasure, while effortlessly dismissing demands or expectations that dare beset her. *Call in the jesters! More soda, more hair-brushing! Tell me for the forty-fourth time today how wonderful I am!*

However, and beware, they'll be other times, more turbulent times, when she'll resist the scepter and its obligations.

In these moments she might act as if she wants to throw off her velvet cape. She'll behave immaturely, make poor choices, kick and scream as if she craves and needs an adult to guide and direct her. But don't be taken in by her drama. Your child doth protest too much. Sure, she'll act all helpless, trying to shift the responsibility for the family and her parenting onto you. But stay tough.

She's almost five now. If she can't make good judgments of her own, and still needs you to assist her decisions and help her to manage her piggy bank, well maybe, just maybe she isn't ready to go to the toy store by herself, much less with her own credit card. And who wants to be ruled by some whining cry-baby?

We all know there are children who thoroughly rule the roost. They reserve the final vote and veto on everything that happens in the home. What the family eats and when. When and with whom the family sleeps. What they watch on television and where the family will go for dinner. Is something amiss when parents want a pizza at Ray's but their toddler insists on that Zagat-rated ($$$$) uptown sushi house?

Some children determine where their parents sit at the table, whether their parents can talk to each other, and where they, the parents, spend every waking moment. I've heard of young children who gave (heeded) advice as to what car or homes their parents should buy. (Does the Beetle come in black-and-red polka dots?)

I know nothing about the reigning Queen Elizabeth's childhood, but I am willing to bet that she was very much a child who knew her place in the home. What does that matter? Not sure, except it'd be ironic if we treat our daughters more like little queens than was true for the real one. I would bet that the English First Family held some belief that, to be a future Queen and good leader, a young girl needed to learn much about responsibility and duty. How, they might have asked themselves, can our young Elizabeth ever lead a kingdom if she herself cannot listen to, respect, and sometimes follow others? Don't our own children deserve parenting no less royal?

12

Onward Parenting Soldier

It's been a couple of days and look at all you've accomplished. You've knelt at the Altar of Parenting where you confessed your spoiling and where you vowed from this day forth to stop it. You've performed your first and bravest deed and shown your child that you are a force to be reckoned with.

You've looked in the mirror and listened to yourself on taped audio. You are no longer asking your child's permission to be the parent. You've realized that it's healthy fun for your child to play Queen. You've decided that it's not healthy for her to actually be Queen.

Like your child's Transformers toys that go from dinosaur to robot, or from villain to hero, you've evolved from Spoiler to Unspoiler. Only your change will not be reversible. While there are many loose ends of your spoiling yet to tie up, those years of days of leniency and overindulgence are coming to a close.

But screenwriters tell us that writing Act II is the toughest. Rather than rely on the big bang of the first act, you will need to sustain and build on its momentum. How, how not?

The writer Anne Lamott describes much of parenting as a roller-coaster ride on which holding on tight is all we can do. Her inviting and engaging prose captures those frightening moments in parenting, moments that can last days, weeks, or longer. As the parent of what are now a college junior and high school senior, I can say that Ms. Lamott knows what she's talking about.

But then again, the fact that parenting can raise the hairs on our necks and gray the hair on our heads does not prove that we are helpless bystanders to our children's childhoods. All through the day, parents take big and small actions to reduce the chaos and uncertainty of their children's lives. And that leads us back to the hows and how nots of your next move.

You are going to try and refrain from fly-by-the-seat-of-your-pants parenting. Much that occurs in a child's day comes suddenly and unexpectedly and corners parents into making rash decisions. The here and now, and its circumstances, can put great pressure on parents to act fast. And so we make decisions—scratch that. And so we react almost by reflex, giving in, saying yes, and doing everything that runs counter to what the parenting angel on our right shoulder is saying we should do. When stressed like that, we run to what's human and natural. We impulsively take the easy and low road (versus the steeper trail that's tougher to hike).

Please, let me be clear. I am not dismissing spontaneous parenting. Anything but. Spontaneity is a wonder in one's daily life. Without it what tedious and joyless zombies might we be for ourselves and others, including the kids. Nor am I suggesting that we parent with the minute-to-minute precision of a space launch.

I am reminding you, however, that you're committed to a war on spoiling. As I've suggested elsewhere—and I'm in danger of overdoing the military metaphor—you need to start thinking a little like a general.

Plan. The best way to avoid reckless spoiling of your child is to anticipate those difficult times when you'll out of the blue be blind-sided by your child's demands or ill-tempered behavior. Imagine how you'd like to attack those situations, and hold it right there in your virtual memory to be summoned when needed. If saying no is hard for you, rehearse. Envision yourself as Meryl Streep playing a mother who, in fact, can say no convincingly.

Think of ways to fight fair. And think of ways to conduct guerilla warfare. Be ready for all of those uncomfortable and unfair dilemmas that your child is certain to create around you. When you mentally prepare for the expectedly unexpected, you'll be less likely to be taken by surprise and less likely to spoil on automatic pilot.

Last, do your planning when you are calm and well behind the front where the battle rages. No parent thinks clearly when firing or being fired upon. Letting your anger fade will help you to

76

avoid saying mean things or acting in ways that hurt more than help. You want to think long-term, not short, avoiding actions that win you a skirmish but lose you the war. Wrestling a toothbrush into your child's mouth, for example, may clean today's plaque, but what will it do for his more lifelong attitude toward health care?

Sometimes, when frustration leads the way, doing nothing will get you farther than acting in haste or out of exasperation. Often, a cool head can be your most able consultant.

13

Everything Is Non-Negotiable

The suspicion, we hope, is planted firmly in your head. *Your child is out to get you.* Not like a hit man or anything, though she can be a saboteur and terrorist in a family way. She has no alternative, perhaps, but to use all of her guile to (try to) get what she wants. What she wants, keep in mind, may be nothing resembling what she (psychologically and developmentally) needs and may even (unconsciously) crave. But she will go for it all the same.

We've also established that she can be, as my father liked to say about me, a Philadelphia lawyer, a pretty cute one in fact (as in conniving). She'll take on any case that centers around herself as plaintiff. How can you beat her at this game, her game?

The simple answer is that you can't. Going head-to-head with your child can be more stacked than playing blackjack at Vegas. Your child will ask for some extra reading at bedtime and, before you know it, she'll be whacking you upside the head with a bait-and-switch that you can't refuse. "Well, if I can't stay up late to have more dessert and play another round of Sorry, then I guess you owe me a back rub and two books before the lights go out."

Where's F. Lee Bailey when you need him?

What began as an innocent-looking request for a little extra playtime stealthily turns into the child's last best ultimatum: "Thirty minutes or forty-five minutes more? What's it going to be?" What's a parent to do? How do you outmaneuver that kind of logic?

The answer is easier said than done. You refuse to negotiate.

Say, for example, you are driving to the grocery store. By the time you park, your child has already asked if he can get some favorite cookies and you've said sure. Nothing wrong with that. We've all been there.

But in the store he soon asks for ice cream, and candy, then wants to critique your shopping up and down 24 aisles. What might that sound like?

"*Why not?*"
"Because I already…"
"*But …*"
"I am not going to say it again."
"*But why not?*"
"I told you once and I …"
"*You bought Ben…*"
"I'm buying you cookies. In fact, I let you pick out two kinds of cookies."
"*But you got Ben's favorite ice cream, not mine…*"
"I'm not saying it again. I can't listen to this the whole time I shop…"
"*But you listen when…*"

You poor parent. I'm getting a headache just writing this scene. So, how can you undo this painful static? Again, you refuse to engage, as in this example:
"*Can I get this ice cream?*"

"I let you pick out cookies."

"*But...*"

The mother calmly walks to the cookie aisle, puts the cookies back on the shelf, and heads to the register.

Okay, I admit it reads pretty smoothly in my four-line scenario. I forgot to mention that the boy throws a whopper of a tantrum. He throws stuff out of the cart and at the register makes an unimaginable ruckus. His mother struggles her way out of the store, feeling such humiliation she swears she'll never be able to shop there again.

And now, I'll take further questions on this hypothetical incident.

Q: What, you ask, could the mother have done when the boy nagged for candy?

A: Better that the mother had returned the cookies when the boy nagged for ice cream and left sooner. And you're right to ask, why'd she let the boy pick out two kinds of cookies when she'd agreed to one? (Keep in mind too that the child

does not need a warning—"If you don't stop..."—
each time the mother is about to set a limit. That
can backfire and teach a child mostly to be a last-
minute reformer. Even as they fight the limit that's
been set, a majority of children will understand
why the parent has done what she has.)

Q: What about when the boy commandeered
his mother's decision-making as to what groceries
to buy?
A: She might have tried to shape the boy's
arguing into an interesting conversation. But,
really, should a six-year-old be the head decider
and be criticizing his mother like that?

Q: Should the mother have punished the boy
when they got home?
A: No need to. Losing his cookies and leaving
the store were the consequences that taught the
child his lesson. (Though the mother can decide
not to take the boy to the next thing he wants to go
to as a consequence for his rudeness in ruining the
shopping trip she needed to go on.)

Q: The mother probably should make both their lives easier and just go shopping without her son. Don't you agree?

A: I could not agree less. These experiences, while trying, are opportunities for both parent and child to learn and build life skills together.

It takes some work to confront your child's demands. "Why can't I play that video game? Alan [his older brother] does!" "You know well what kind of games you can play. Push me again on this one and your Xbox goes away for a week." But your child will have to push again. How will she otherwise know that you mean it? She'll keep pushing and repeating this pattern until she's convinced you are serious.

14

Follow Through

You seem to be doing very well. Let's take this quiz and see for sure.

You are walking from the pediatrician's office to the car. Your child asks you to stop to browse the local toy store that opened yesterday. What do you say?

(a) "Great idea! We can see what new toys they've brought in since we browsed there yesterday."

(b) "Absolutely. You did such a great job waiting five minutes for your brother that you deserve something very special."

(c) You check your wallet. "Okay, I guess. But I only have forty dollars. Are you sure you don't want to wait until I can get more money?"

(d) "I was hoping you'd ask."

You can't come up with an answer? And why not? Ah, you are very clever and correct. Indeed, the answer is (e) All of the above. (Please forgive my sarcasm.)

Nowhere is follow-through more needed than in your parenting (except in bowling, maybe). Recall the last chapter and how you said you would put the Xbox away where it couldn't be used? Did you ever even move it?

Like idle hands and minds, idle threats can be dangerous. What do they teach? The obvious, that we talk big and blow a lot of hot air. When we don't follow through it's as if we word process documents that we neglect to save. Without that save button our work disappears as if it never existed.

How could I imagine following through in the instance of the Xbox? Normally a parent would want to make some noise—you know, angrily whipping the plug out of the wall, grabbing the Xbox by one hand, and storming out of the house. (Kind of like throwing the TV out the window.) But I'd do it differently. Later that evening, when the child falls asleep, I'd quietly remove the computer to a safe place.

I am not trying to be sneaky and I don't fear the child's knowing. I want the removal to be unceremonious and not at all in the child's face. My wish is to avoid a major confrontation that will do more harm than good. I am not trying to humiliate or overpower the child, nor do I wish to set up a situation in which I end up playing tug-o'-war with the Xbox or, worse, physically battling.

The next morning or afternoon, when the child goes to play with the Xbox, it won't be there. "Where's my Xbox?" she'll cry. You'll tell her it is gone for now and that you'll return it in several days or perhaps a week. Your child may scream, protest, and tell you why you can't do this to her. "It's mine," she'll yell. Or, she'll fall apart and wail. "You don't love me!"

Think of her cries as the Sirens' call. Knowing that he couldn't resist their seductive cries, Ulysses ordered his men to tie him to the ship's mast. How will you resist your child's drama? If anything, her tirade should persuade you that your decision to unspoil your child is warranted.

During that week of abstinence, your child will try to earn, cajole, flatter, charm, and intimidate early release of the Xbox. She may appear to have learned her lesson. How easy it would be for you to break down and bring it out prematurely. *Don't!*

Giving in on the fifth or sixth day can teach your child to scratch and claw until the final gasp (and when a child is busy clawing she usually isn't doing much reckoning and reflecting). Think of your child as having committed a crime that carries a minimum sentence of seven days. Seven-day sentences must be served. If your conviction in her conviction is certain and assured, her frantic attempts to undo it, however noisy and robust, will seem meager, transparent, and easy to ignore.

And when it's time to bring the video game back, clearly state the expectations you will hold from that day on. Your child may judge that she's finally getting back what is rightfully hers. But you can straighten her out on this one. The video game represents a privilege and you, as her parent, should know what behavior deserves such a reward. And if she misbehaves in the same way as before, don't hesitate to press the replay button, doing the whole business again, maybe for longer.

As you've noticed, I have stayed away from mentioning specific ages. It varies. Younger children learn best over shorter time periods, perhaps hours or a day. School-aged children often need lengthier consequences to feel their sting and to reform their attitude. But there are few hard and fast rules. Some teens need only a raised eyebrow; some toddlers need a parental version of Alcatraz.

What kinds of things can parents take away?

Anything electronic. Computers, video games, cell phones, music players, televisions, and personal DVD players. For younger children, any kind of toys, though I'd never ever take their teddy bears or blankies.

Oh, and last, when you do return whatever it was you took away, please don't do something special to make it up to your child. You went through all that hardship in order to provide your child something she needs to grow up well. That was a loving act. You owe your child nothing more. Are you willing to gamble all that away out of your lingering guilt or discomfort over being a parent with authority?

15

Like Taking Snow from an Eskimo

Well, that title says it all, doesn't it? And it anticipates, I suppose, what some parents thought toward the end of the last chapter. What do you take away when you can't seem to think of something appropriate to take away or your child seems not to care? And what do you do when she claims she doesn't care?

Let's do the last question first. When children declare that they don't care, that is almost always an indicator of just the opposite, that they do care. Children who don't care don't bother to say it out loud. So, we as parents ignore their pleas of not caring, reminding ourselves that they do care and watching that their pretense doesn't derail or slow our best efforts to unspoil them.

The first question is more difficult. How do parents find consequences that wield sufficient power to reach their children? Is there any value in taking an Xbox from a child who also owns or has access to a Nintendo Wii and PlayStation, not to mention assorted handheld video games? (Find something better or hijack the whole load.)

In my practice I have over and over seen parents take away electronic equipment from children who cope by doubling their use of other electronic toys. Take away video games, they play computer games. Take away the computer, they watch movies and TV. (It's worrisome, and does imply a bit of the addict's desperation, don't you think?)

The question what then does a parent take away is critical but first demands a quick side trip. Those parents I just mentioned, the ones who in vain seem to always take away electronics, often express utter bewilderment as to what else they could use to "punish" their child. And yet, though it never seems to work, they take it away, take it away, take it away once more—which brings me to the point of this little joy ride.

Forget about being a one-trick pony. I don't care if you can walk a tightrope on two legs while juggling fiery swords and bowling balls with your arms. Stick with one trick and you aren't going to last in any circus. Wondrously effective one-trick parenting strategies eventually grow weary and predictable.

Parenting is a set of skills that we can learn and get better at. Experiment with new techniques and study the effects they have on your child. When you discover methods that work, fine-tune them for specific situations. Consider yourself a kind of tennis star who must be ready for the variety of shots your child will serve you.

And just as parents need a repertoire of unspoiling strategies, they need a range of things to take away. It can't always be the same thing, especially a thing that the child can readily live without. In fact, it doesn't have to be a thing. It can be an activity or an experience.

If your child treats you terribly all day, do you really feel like taking her to T-ball practice? Even if you're willing to take her, should you? When I suggest to parents the possibility of withholding a sports activity from their child, they recoil. "But getting outside is good for her." "What will I tell her coach?" "Oh, great. She'll get exactly what she wants. She hates swim practice."

Sounds like a confusing mess. But confusing messes can be sorted through, teased apart, and straightened out. If your child will be thrilled to miss that sport, then it's not a good consequence. Keep looking.

If your child doesn't deserve to go to sports that day, tell the coach you are working on some issues with your child. He or she is probably a parent, too. (And it's not as if your child is a salaried athlete playing professional sports.)

If you and your child feel that she will be letting the team down, all the more reason to use that consequence. It is obviously something she cares about.

If you feel that the team needs your child for a game, then delay the consequence, and keep her from going to the next practice or two after that game. Recall, be creative.

Parents can use the same reasoning to devise consequences involving dance rehearsals, music lessons, and birthday parties. (Get back on your chair. Yes, I said birthday parties.) Though I recognize many parents won't go this far.

What to do at the restaurant where a bratty child can come to life? You know how miserable that can be. I've had several parents solve that problem by planning a ruined night out.

They go for dinner to a usual and cheap place, their child's favorite, where they know their child will act miserably. While waiting for the food to come, the parents patiently endure the same old, same old. A few seconds after the food arrives, before the child has time to eat more than a bite, and without a warning, the parents up and leave. They neither reprimand the child nor bring the food home. They don't yell and they don't punish. They merely go home.

It works.

It can work as well at the movies. Leave thirty minutes or more into a good movie, one the child likes.

You're right, it is hugely inconvenient. It means wasting time, wasting money, and maybe making both parents and siblings suffer unfairly when they aren't the ones misbehaving. Then again, remember where you're aiming. Are you trying to annoy your family? Are you trying to be provocative?

No, you are trying to unspoil your child. And that is more important than basketball, Shrek, and chicken nuggets all wrapped together.

16

Get It Together

When it comes to parenting, some couples really get their groove going. They share the same values and expectations. They each had good parents of their own who taught them good ways to raise children. With the seamless synchrony of Viennese waltzers, they parent together, alternatively, and side by side as if they'd choreographed and rehearsed every step. Each parent feels supported and never undermined by the other parent. Each seems to watch the other's parenting back with a sixth sense.

But you and I and most everyone else I know are not that blessed and golden parenting couple. Nor were Mr. and Mrs. W.

Whenever we met it was the same. Mrs. W. shamefully avowed the spoiling she'd done. "I bought them gum anyway." "I can't believe it myself, I still took them to the fair." "Even after all they'd done, I made them brownies." After each confession Mr. W. rolled his eyes, shook his head, and rubbed his brow in disapproval.

Mr. W. would ever say something like, "She just doesn't get it." Then, with Mrs. W leading the way, we'd problem-solve helping her to not spoil the children who were considerably out of control. But some sessions later, a bigger and different truth came out.

"How could you let the three of them do that? I don't understand," Mrs. W. said with visible upset. Mr. W. looked at the floor. "I let myself get a job for one lousy Saturday and now I have to worry that I can't leave the house?"

Through tears Mrs. W. described coming home to find a mess beyond belief. Nacho cheese and ketchup on the new couch. Spilled soda, the cans lying on their sides. Model glue on the table. Paint on the rug. "I'd just cleaned the whole house on Friday!"

"They're boys," Mr. W. defended himself.

But Mrs. W. knew all about boys. She mothered three of them and she'd grown up with brothers. She was a bona fide expert on boys' curiosity, energy, and adventurousness. But she wasn't dealing with boys will be boys. This was Huckleberry Finn meets the seed of Chuckie, times three.

"You're worse than the boys!" she accused.

"You have no idea what it's like being with them for a whole day," Mr. W. blurted.

It took several minutes of silence and tension, before the two of them broke into laughter.

"I don't know how she does it." Mr. W. looked at the ceiling. "It's too much for me."

Forget what *Redbook* says about candles and satin sheets, there's absolutely nothing more seductive in a relationship than blaming the Other.

Remember, it often takes two to spoil. Just as it usually takes two to unspoil. Don't be fooled into thinking you are the (good parent) unspoiler and your Other is the (bad parent) spoiler. It's nearly always more complicated. In general, the parent who does the lion's share of caretaking and nurturing is prone to indulge more, especially when worn out. Beware of critiquing the Other until you've tried doing what she or he does for a few weeks, day in and day out.

Remember also that spoiling can be a natural extension of loving and good parenting. True, you'd prefer your well-loved child to be less spoiled (and that's why you're reading this book). On the other hand, you would never want your child raised in an unspoiling home void of love, warmth, giving, and pleasure.

If, upon scrutiny and honest self-appraisal, you assess that you are truly the healthily unspoiling parent, then you want to do all you can to support and win your Other over to your unspoiling way of life. (I say "healthily" to distinguish you from a parent whose stern, joyless, and withholding brand of unspoiling is more worrisome than good.) We know, for sure, that blame and criticism probably won't be the way to succeed in your mission. And—do I have to say it?—let's always remember that the laws of spoiling and unspoiling apply equally to all parenting couples, whatever their race, religion, sexual orientation, or marital status.

17

Some Not-ABCs for Their Ps and Qs

Your list of do's has grown longer and more flexible. You have much to feel good about. Hold off, though, on that hammock and beer. There's work to be done. In this chapter we pay tribute to those former familiar ways of parenting, the ones that originally contributed to your child's being spoiled. Herein we salute a hit parade sampling of parenting don'ts.

Those ways, essentially habits, won't just quietly fade into the sunset. Parenting habits die hard. Like dormant viruses, they lay in waiting, ready to pounce when you are weak, tired, and overwhelmed. Let's revisit these basics of how *not* to parent.

Counting to three. Now there's an effective technique. It gets toddlers to snap to until they soon enough realize they don't have to.

Don't make me get to three. Or...

Or what? Or then you'll really be lost as to what to do with me? Or you'll be so frustrated you'll only have giving in or hitting me as options? Or you'll have to keep counting to a million?

Two and seven-eighths, two and...

Hey, do any of you parents have a calculator I can borrow?

Time-outs are a mixed bag. They can provide children and parents valuable space to separate and cool down. Used briefly and wisely they can help a child to regroup. My experience says that time-outs are many a parent's single parenting trick. They are often used indiscriminately. They can leave young children feeling abandoned and ashamed, like that turn-of-the-century child sitting in the corner wearing a dunce cap. A young child can reflect on what she did for only so long, usually a handful of minutes. Like the Genie left for centuries in the bottle, children who spend too much time in time-outs risk growing mostly angry and vengeful.

"But you promised!"

We adore our children and want to give them everything. We want to promise them the moon even though we know that we'll never be able to give it to them. Watch any old movie and see what love can make a person promise.

But what does it feel like to be repeatedly promised what is never delivered? And where does that leave you, the promiser? Your reputation will precede you. You will disappoint. And you will be accused. Liar!

You can promise as much as you'd like to always love your child. But, ask yourself, why does she need you to promise what you'll buy her tomorrow or where you'll take her or whether you'll be home when you say you will? Maybe you have a bigger problem to take care of.

Why do you make promises when what you really mean to say is *no,* or *we'll see, I'm not deciding now*?

Why do you make promises when you know there's a good chance you'll break them?

"Do you want to put on the blue or the green pajamas?"

Rather than struggle over every one of the countless moments in a toddler's day, parents came up with an ingenious notion. Offer two choices that you, the parent, can live with—in this case blue pajamas or green pajamas. The concept behind the idea wasn't bad. It seemed to hold the potential for achieving two important goals: (1) what you want (getting him dressed) and (2) what he wants (doing it his way).

This device worked like a charm. Until, being creatures of (bad) habit, parents overdid it. They asked their children to choose everything, And the children, being clever creatures, caught on.

When the parent says: "Do you want to put on the blue or the green pajamas?" the parent *means*: "You are putting on pajamas, so which ones do you choose?"

The child *hears*: "Do you want to put on pajamas now, later, or not at all? It's up to you."

Parents so relied on this linguistic strategy that they lost their muscle for making decisions and exercising authority. They also got so used to asking that they forgot how to just state a demand. "Let's get going" devolved to "Shall we get going?" Asking a four-year-old whether she wants to go to childcare today doesn't make sense when you have to be at work in an hour. Especially when you know she'd prefer to stay home.

Leave wheeler-dealing and Door No. 3 to the Game Show Network where it belongs.

Despite our attempts to be perfect parents, we'll occasionally hurt our children or let them down. We make mistakes like everyone else. We can't help being human, but we can make it up to our kids.

Thank goodness that one of our largest toy store chains had the foresight to print money just for this situation. Though a giraffe's head sits where Lincoln's should, the money is good in most every state and thirty-five countries. There's no richer feeling than watching your child's crying face light up when you pull out a two-inch wad of giraffe money.

"There you go!" you say with a wink and pizzaz as you squeeze a couple of twenties into your young child's palm. "Get whatever you want." Your sincere generosity will instantly win back your child's heart and teach him a valuable lesson on how to manipulate people.

(Oops, this strategy was supposed to go in my other book, *How to Ruin Your Child*. What to really do when you err? Face it, admit it, apologize—and if necessary, work on not doing it again—all the while staying that strong, caring, and unspoiling parent.)

Oh, and need I add, Why would you ever, ever (did I say ever?) give in to or respond to a child when he is whining or screaming at you?

"I'll be able to hear you better when you talk in a regular voice."

Children hate not being listened to. Calmly stay put and your child will tone down, fast. Think about it. He doesn't whine or yell at his teachers.

106

I'm willing to bet that you could come up with your own list of parenting taboos. I'm willing to bet you could advise plenty of other parents on how not to spoil their child. Kind of ironic, isn't it?

18

Unspoiling Solo

Well, if it really does take a village to raise a child, where does that leave the single parent (the great majority of whom are single mothers)? Any married parent knows way too many moments of total exhaustion, discouragement, and despair. Can those coupled parents imagine for a second what it might be like to do it alone, to know that no spouse is going to come and relieve them in a few hours or even the next day? Some single mothers singlehandedly parent their children not just for a few months or years, but for their entire childhoods.*

---

*I recognize there are fathers who also parent alone and to whom this discussion applies.

What must it be like to do it all by yourself? My many years of clinical work have taught me that, however they got there, single parents have the toughest job on earth. And because they do it alone, some are especially vulnerable to spoiling their children. Consider the good reasons why.

Foremost, they are physically exhausted. Nothing weakens a parent's resolve like pure fatigue. Parenting straight ahead is tough enough when we're running on all cylinders with our tanks full. Try doing it when you haven't had enough rest since you can't remember when. When you do it alone, there's no one to pass the parenting baton on to. When your child is sick, as just one small instance, it doesn't matter that you also have the flu. You're still the on-duty nurse.

Many single parents are emotionally spent. Parenting children can suck us dry. Those of us who are married can turn to our spouses for support and renewal. Our spouses can listen to and maybe even confirm our frustrations. In the best of times they'll remind us that we are doing the right thing or help us to get there. And then there are the little huge things they do, such as feeding, nurturing, touching, and loving us when life and parenting are doing us in. Some single parents face what can be the unrelenting drudgery and daunting crises of parenting with neither a hand to hold nor a shoulder to cry on.

Then, there are those big and little parenting decisions. Parenting and unspoiling require a lot of thought and deliberation. Single mothers can be isolated and have no ready person to bounce their ideas and reasoning off. Consider how many executives contribute to decision-making in the corporate and business worlds. Talk about a diffusion of responsibility. Single parents bear it all upon their backs. Few parents who are married will take responsibility for 100 percent of their parenting choices. In fact, it can almost be a reflex for many married parents to push decisions onto the Other and then blame them when it doesn't work out perfectly. (Of course, I've only heard about this dynamic. I would never myself do anything like that.) Many single mothers have no one there to tell them, You're doing okay right now, right here.

Oh, and then there's that awful guilt. Guilt maybe because they are doing it alone, because, in the case of single mothers, there is no husband and father. We all know the kinds of things that guilt can make us do. Guilt can drive single parents to routinely enable late bedtimes, give gifts that are undeserved or that they can't afford, and excuse misbehavior they know to be inexcusable. That same guilt can also motivate single mothers to neglect their own needs. (I assume, by now, that married readers have noted that they may share much of the single mother's experience.)

What can single parents do to counter these stressful pressures toward spoiling?

- ❖ Get rest, eat well, exercise, and tend to your health.
- ❖ Find and nurture healthy relationships—with friends, family, or potential partners—that offer good ears and a welcome shoulder.

- ❖ Use trusted others to help sound and sort out your parenting decisions and philosophy.
- ❖ Build places for fun, joy, and self-nurturing in your life.

As Cheryl Erwin and I wrote in *How to Turn Boys into Men Without a Man Around the House*, we are not naïve enough to believe you will now "put yourself at the front of the line. We know it will be your [child's] hunger that you feed before your own and his scrape that you bandage while your own cut bleeds. That is a mother's way. We just hope that you will work at making your own well-being a higher priority—if not for your sake, for your [child's]."

19

Spare the Rod

I don't believe that children need to be hit to grow right. In fact, hitting children carries many risks. But sparing children from discipline is a mistake and contributes to their being spoiled and uncivilized.

Children need to learn where they end and where others begin. Limits are the foundation for a child's being able to control himself and live harmoniously in a home and community.

Consider what limits do. They...

- ❖ keep children safe
- ❖ keep parents, peers, and others safe
- ❖ keep the home and property safe
- ❖ make clear to children what is acceptable and what isn't

❖ show that their parents can handle the children's angry and rejecting reactions

❖ lay the foundation for children to grasp the rules and laws outside of the home— at school, on the playground, and in society

❖ strengthen children's self-control and patience

❖ teach children to channel their stronger impulses into play and words (rather than into destructive anger and violence)

❖ show children that their parents don't fear taking on the duties of a parent

Limits demonstrate to children that they are separate individuals in a world of people. "No, you can't go through my pocketbook. That's mine!" "That's your brother's cupcake. You have your own." "No, we're not raising the heat. If you're cold, you can put on a sweater. Everyone else in the family is warm." (Of course, if the child is ill or something, turning up the thermostat might be a moment of good indulgence.)

Limits also include the notion of boundaries and privacy. It is healthy for parents to have privacy in their bedrooms when they choose. Many toddlers have free run of their parents' bedrooms, offices, cell phones, and laptops. (I hate observing parents awkwardly trying to extricate their phones from their child's grasp.) That your limits make your child feel so totally angry and shut out speaks to the heart of the problem. Children need to grow used to handling such reasonable limits without feeling devastated, rejected, and unloved.

And what about your personal space? Why, anyway, do you want your child with you every minute? Your child needs to learn how, for example, to share a chair without merging and without climbing down your blouse or up your skirt. It happens more than you know. Don't wait for your child's groping fingers to grab your earrings or poke your nostrils. Set her down. "You can sit with me, but I don't like being poked. It hurts." Your words and actions will momentarily sting her. But when she tries again, your warm welcome and steadfast limits will soon help her to find a more comfortable place on or near your lap.

As I and pretty much everyone else have said before, children need love and *discipline*. Though this is a book about unspoiling and not child discipline, let me briefly offer some guidelines.

Discipline fairly. Do not heap discipline all on one child. Don't rev your child up, then punish her for getting wild. Are you a parent who lives life at seventy-five miles per hour and then erupts when your overstimulated child finally gets to you? Watch that your discipline is in line with the crime. Countering your child's snowball with a barrage of cannonballs will anger and hurt your child more than instill anything good in her.

Discipline reasonably. Take ample responsibility for the disciplinary state of your child and home. It is not your child's fault that you don't set adequate limits. It is not her fault that you (try to) use a loud voice as your primary parenting tool. Strive not to discipline because you are frustrated, irritable, or having a bad day. Discipline when there's good reason to.

Discipline consistently. By consistently I mean that the same offense will on the average get the same disciplinary reaction from you, and that it will happen regularly. Consistent discipline does not require robotic precision. Nor do two parents or caretakers have to be in perfect synchrony.

Parents can undermine one another and a home of mixed messages can wreak havoc on children. For example, what does a child think and feel when one parent repeatedly says "no dessert" and the other parent serves up more ice cream, or worse, when his parents fight aloud over every parenting decision?

More often and for children's benefit, parenting couples complement rather than replicate each other's disciplining. One is hands-off, the other is a micro-manager. One is sterner, one is more lenient. In a shared balance of power, such dynamic duos play off each other and expose children to a broader variety of parenting styles and experience.

Discipline judiciously. Parents don't need to put on black robes and powdered wigs nor should they assume an arrogance of power. By judicious I suggest parenting that is thoughtful and well reasoned. Judicious parents seek to understand their parenting. They aspire to discipline in ways that are sound, opportune, and effective. Instead of obsessing on their mistakes, they ponder what they've learned and search for new possibilities.

They aim to make the most good of their discipline and to avoid discipline that is useless or harmful.

Discipline compassionately. Compassion is your disciplinary ace up your sleeve. Parents misbelieve that disciplinary action must be backed up with anger and intimidation. "Now you've done it!" said with a scowl and some heat.

I'm not suggesting we hide our genuine disapproval. For many young children, seeing their parents' honest reactions helps to develop a sturdy conscience. Potent limits and consequences, however, don't require parents to pile on the anger. Once you've set a limit and stuck to it, let your kindness and empathy show. Don't forget to leave room for your child's authentic feelings over having been disciplined (and having messed up). Let her apologize and make amends. Let her cry, and let your sons cry. Limits and discipline help our children be the kind of children that bring out the best in us. By helping our children to behave, we are helping them be children for whom we can ever sustain our good feelings, empathy, and respect.

20

Blue Ribbon Losers

Am I calling our children losers? I know, I agree. How can I say such a thing? But it holds more than a shred of truth. We've been turning our children into blue ribbon losers. Don't believe me? Look at the statistics on teen anxiety, depression, alcohol and drug use, cheating, suicide, self-injury, and so on.

The eminently wise education writer Alfie Kohn makes the case convincingly. Young children work to please their parents. They strive to do things that will elicit their parents' approving smiles and warm glow of pride. These children will work for stickers and gold seals that say "job well done." Over time these external rewards become part of the children's inside, so that they want to do well to please themselves. They will naturally come to value their own learning and achievements because of the good ways it makes them feel and by experiencing the bigger rewards their efforts earn. (See Kohn's *Punished by Rewards*, 1999.)

Gaining the approval of others is part of children's growing. We never stop needing some of that. But we have to find a way to get over our compulsive need to celebrate—meaning *reward, note, confirm, spotlight*—every step the child takes, whether big or little, accomplished or failed, new or old, well earned or earned by happenstance. We are creating a generation of children who cannot live without the constant spotlight, without someone on the outside forever stamping what they do as worthwhile and grand.

At what age do children start to roll their eyes when they get trophies for sports they dislike and for which they've never produced a drop of sweat? Go to any piano recital and see all the Beethoven and Mozart medals that are awarded. There's an entire cottage industry built around our obsession. Go online and peek at these thick catalogs featuring an infinite assortment of prizes disguised as plastic key rings, frappe cups, and retractable pens.

But the bone I'm picking is not with coaches or music teachers. At least they can point to a body of work deserving note—the child came to a season of soccer or practiced piano daily for a year. Contrast that with the body of work that parents are prone to honor.

"Wow, you did a great job brushing your teeth."

"Wow, you did a great job eating lunch."

"Wow, you're having so much fun playing with that new toy." *Thanks for telling me, otherwise I would not have noticed.*

"Wow, what a great job you did sleeping."

"Wow, you did a great job picking up those blocks. And Daddy only asked eleven times!"

"Wow, you did a great job inhaling oxygen and exhaling carbon dioxide. We are so proud of you!"

Listen to parents at the playground. Complimenting their children has become as much second nature as breathing.

"Wow, you drank all your juice."

"Wow, you climbed so high."

"Wow, you really pushed that kid off the jungle gym."

"Wow, you really kicked my leg."

"Hey, wait a minute, that hurt. What am I saying?"

Okay, I made my point. But this is a big problem and one carrying harm for your child. It is also a problem that can be handily discharged and remedied. How?

Foremost, change your mind-set. Does anyone notice and praise your every step and breath? Why, barely anyone notices that you hobble through the house with a broken foot. Life is tough. A child who's addicted to perpetual celebration will suffer much in a world that will often be busy with other things and people.

Does this mean you should ignore your child? Not at all. It means reserving praise for worthy achievement, most of all achievement that required effort. Your child does not need to get a prize for being able to decide between two toys in less than half an hour. He doesn't need a reward for not biting the cat.

But he does deserve notice and validation for trying hard to be and do better.

"Wow, your little sister just grabbed your new toy. And you didn't even hit her."

"Wow, you tried to put your dish in the dishwasher just like we do."

"Wow, you shut off that video game even though you wanted to keep playing. That must have been hard." He doesn't need flattery for being good. But he will appreciate your taking notice when he tries.

See it though your child's eyes. He is trying to get past something, learn a new skill, or give up a misbehavior. The last thing he needs is to be spoiled more when he is trying to get less spoiled. *Even brats hate being brats.* Restrain your urge to reward his struggle with things or praise. Instead of rewarding the product of his effort verify the effort itself. "I can see you're trying very hard to keep your temper." That is what he's doing, and that, if anything, is what he wants validated.

Some parents claim success with another method. Fifty dollars for each A grade, thirty dollars per B, and fifteen dollars per C with a seventy-five dollar bonus for making the honor roll. Other parents disagree with the whole idea of paying your child cash for grades. They much prefer to give a small token of acknowledgment, a symbolic gesture, something like the U2-commemorative iPod or a vintage Stratocaster.

How about a different kind of gift? Something like: "Wow, it must feel good to see all your hard work pay off."

To be able to say such a thing, you have to take your child's perspective, remember all her studying, and leave yourself out of the equation, allowing the report card and all that it represents to be hers alone. What a selfless and generous gift for a parent to give a child!

21

Work It, Work Them

As the previous chapter showed, much of the self-esteem movement has proved disastrous. Parents mistakenly believed that if they bathed their children in love and admiration they would thrive as adults who deep inside ever felt thoroughly wonderful and worthy. But they didn't create contented, productive, self-glowing individuals. Just the opposite. We now know that constant stroking doesn't build good esteem as much as it barely maintains esteem that's shaky and in need of constant buttressing.

It's actually a strong sense of competency that endows a child with hardy esteem. How does a parent foster a child's sense of competency? By creating opportunities for that child to face and master challenges. These challenges do not have to be enormous, however.

We are not talking Mount Everest or memorizing the dictionary. I refer to the challenges that comprise what most of us take to be everyday life.

Learning to walk, to put on one's own socks, to use the potty, and to sleep in a crib are early aspects of that natural drive to do for oneself. "Mommy, I brushed my own teeth." Many parents look at their seemingly helpless teenagers and wonder where all that prideful independence vanished. (But you've got a few years till then.)

Let your child assert her independence and follow her lead. If she asks for help putting a red piece on her LEGO creation, refrain from adding the green, blue, and black. Want to see indignation in the raw? Help a young child more than she wants to be helped. Grrrrrrr!

When a growing child asks for help, it is usually because she is stuck and frustrated and wants just enough assistance so that she can speedily get back on her adventure of self-actualization. So, one way that we foster a sense of competence is by staying out of the way, trying not to block the child's innate drive toward mastery and autonomy.

We guide her, for example, making sure she doesn't hurt herself with knives or kitchen gadgetry when attempting to make us breakfast. Yet we don't squash or in any way demoralize her forward march and earnest ambition. Want to see utter frustration and disappointment? When your child clumsily tries to clean up a milk spill using the new dustmop, scream at him, "Just get out. You're only making it worse." Ouch.

Let your child make repairs and amends should be a parenting commandment.

How else can parents nurture a sense of competency? By not interrupting natural consequences.

What are examples of natural consequences?

- ❖ A child who refuses to wear his hat feels cold.
- ❖ A child who out of anger rejects her dinner is hungry later on.
- ❖ A child who gobbles all of her popcorn has to watch her brother eat his popcorn all through the show.

❖ A child who breaks his new toy truck in a rage has to play without it.

Sounds simple, but it isn't. Most parents have a compulsive instinct to save their children from the natural consequences of their actions. We'll do plenty of yelling and blaming, but then we'll undo it all and make sure our children are well protected from seeing or feeling the consequences their actions have wrought. We'll buy them more cookies, popcorn, and a new truck. What is it about letting our children feel and live with those consequences that frightens us?

Unless they are in danger, let the children stew in the messes they make.

As your child grows older and has run-ins with the outside world, you may want to run alongside him like some bodyguard or guardian angel. We all understand that wish. Then I ask, "How can your child grow strong and able unless she learns to handle life?"

Think of it. A child feels a little criticized by her teacher. My parents would have asked me what

I'd done wrong and then gone back to what they were doing. As I look back, I realize they endowed me with a trust that I could manage my own life.

What message does the slightly disgruntled child get when she watches her parents take her side against her teacher and run to the school with lawyer in hand? Whatever happened to "She's your teacher. Work it out."

How do we sabotage a child's burgeoning sense of competency? We rescue her from her responsibilities. We do her homework. We run interference for her at school. We do her chores, then underwrite her going to the movies anyway.

We buy her toys on layaway and allow her to never pay us back. We undermine and bad mouth coaches and other grownups on the outside who attempt to hold her accountable.

Why don't we just cut off her arms and legs?

22

Thank You, Thank You Very Much

"Why...you...you...ungrateful little..." Why do those words come out so glibly and feel so satisfying to say, even on a keyboard? We all feel it, I think. Parents love their children so much and give so much, there is almost nothing their children can do to show their gratitude. But that is in the world of feelings.

There's no reason that children should express that kind of thanks. Nor do they owe us anything. We had children. It is their growing up well that is our reward, just as it will be for them with their children. Nonetheless, I pose the question, what can parents do when their children seem to feel and show no appreciation for anything in their lives?

This question raises yet another and deeper question: What, beyond reasons of temperament and constitution, can cause a child not to feel gratitude? Though you can't feel it, we are now churning in the eye of the spoiling hurricane.

Children who get and get no matter what tend to appreciate less. They tend to take it all for granted. You may have bought me the world yesterday but what have you done for me lately? *I don't know. Let me see if Venus is for sale.*

I am an adult who appreciates much. My wife is the same. Our families and childhoods were as different as can be. The added fact that she grew up in wealthy Long Island and I grew up in a working class city outside of Boston doesn't seem to matter. Together we've asked ourselves, "Why do we tend to feel fortunate and thankful for what we get?" The only answer we've come up with is that neither of us got a whole lot. There's nothing like not getting to make a person appreciate what they get.

It makes sense. Skip breakfast and lunch and your dinner is bound to taste great. Save up for a year to buy a baseball glove and you will not forget to bring it home from the field. But get a truckload of presents for Christmas and by New

Year's Day you won't remember what you got. You might even have started a new list.

I know, we can't go back to how it was and I'm not sure that it would be a good thing even if we could. I do know that we—our kids and ourselves—are both victims of a consumer society that is sinister and out of control. How does a parent resist all that, defy corporate America, and not keep up with the Joneses? I wish I knew. Become Amish?

What I know is that our economy has changed since I was a boy. People step over pennies and children say cute things like "It's only forty-five dollars." Try to find a kid to mow your lawn. How can we teach our children to know the value of a dollar, saving, and financial prudence?

Refuse to buy them sneakers that cost six times the price of your own work shoes. Refuse to give them absolute free rein on an expensive menu, especially when they never eat what they order. Refuse to give them allowances that resemble salaries. Insist that they live within the budgets of that allowance. Resist buying them so much and start to notice how many things—toys, clothes, downloadable songs, and snacks—you buy them in a week. (There's a good bet it's at least ten times what you were given at the same age.)

What else can you do? Teach them how to work. Instilling a work ethic starts early, well before your child has the physical strength, ability, and sense to help in any significant way. Capitalize on your young child's eagerness to be mommy's or daddy's little helper. Invite your toddler to help you around the house. Let her hold onto the vacuum or hammer beside your hand. Let her help to put away the groceries. As she grows, show her what she can do and give her reasonable tasks. Make helping you an enjoyable and satisfying time, not one of criticism and perfectionism. At a young age require that she perform age-appropriate chores, not for pay but as her contribution to the family. Eventually, some parents tie those increasingly demanding chores to her allowance.

Children who learn to like working at a young age tend to carry that good feeling and personal commitment within themselves throughout their adolescence and lifetime. They will on their own seek out more responsibility as their maturing bodies and minds enable them to. Be careful that your affluence does not dissuade you from creating conditions for your child to want to work. For that would be depriving them of valuable education.

With all that we can do, are we wrong for still wanting just a little TLC and a few nods for all we do as parents? Surely not. Meanwhile, learn to take heart from the little things. Note the baby steps that your once disorderly son has taken on the road to civilized neatness. Take pride in the way that your daughter helped the neighbors in their time of need (even if it is kindness that's yet to come your way). Smile at the way your children put aside the noisy fracas long enough to set the table without your having had to ask. Celebrate them to yourself and take credit for the change. Way to go, *Unspoiler*!

Yes, there will be occasional moments of true epiphany, rites of passage at which your children's good and unspoiled growth will astound you. And there may even be signs of gratitude along the way.

For most parents, however, the true thank yous will come much later when they, our children, are grown up and maybe have their own families. We'll look at the good and decent people they have become and we'll know as sure as anything that what we did was appreciated and worth it.

23

Take a Bow

Well, you've done it. By now your child should be looking a lot more like the child you were thinking of parenting. And maybe when you look in the mirror, you are looking a little more like that parent you wanted to be.

By now you've probably caught on to my little secret. There really is no such thing as unspoiling. In fact, there's really no such word. But don't be mad at me. My ploy meant no harm and was full of the best intention.

If on the first page I'd told you the simple truth, I fear you wouldn't have given me and my method a fair shake. I fear you would not have believed that you could really unspoil your child. There, I'm doing it again.

So what's the big secret?

Unspoiling is nothing more than the absence of spoiling. You didn't have to go back and undo three, four, maybe eight years of spoiling. All you had to do was to stop your spoiling from now on.

But I suspected that if I'd said that, you would not have taken me seriously. I still fear that you think it couldn't be that simple. But it is. You see, children, thank goodness, are not like fruit. They don't overripen and turn bad. They keep growing. Nature sees to it.

And children, being hopeful, seek to grow better. They sometimes sound as if they give up on their parents and themselves; they seldom do. They are always searching for the parenting they crave and need, parenting that sets limits and expectations and that refuses to spoil them.

You have been working hard to change, and no one recognizes that more than your child. Keep at it. Allow both yourself and your child to change, to do better, to be better. And let the past mistakes go. Consider yourself a spoiler no more.

Of course, you've noticed that there was much about parenting (and spoiling) that I never covered.

That was the price of my wanting my message to come through loud and clear, short and sweet. You get the big picture now. There are bookshelves of good books that can help you solve new or different problems, including spoiling or any other aspect of parenting.

What matters is that you now know you can do it. If you can unspoil your child, you can do anything as a parent. It's true.

As life goes on, there'll be many things you'll come to regret. I can promise you, however—and, yes, I do mean promise—unspoiling your child will not be one of them.

NOTES

NOTES

NOTES

NOTES

NOTES

Index

Getting too much, effects of, 135-137
Grades, paying for child's, 127-128
Gratitude, child's, 135-137
Guilt, 58, 59
Giving into child, risks of, 65-66
Grabbing child's attention, 25-29
Grand (unspoiling) gesture, 25-29
  why it works, 35-39

Help-giving, 130-131

I don't care, 91

Keeping up with the Joneses, 137
Kohn, A., 123-124

Lamott, A., 74
Limits,
  child's need for, 23
  functions of, 115-117
  lack of, 50-52
  setting, 52-53, 80-84

Motivation to unspoil, parents', 18, 41-47
Movies, leaving the, 29, 95

A Word of Caution

This book can help most any home and family. But it can't do everything. Problems that involve abuse, drugs, or alcohol require the special help of counselors, therapy, self-help groups, etc. Even should this book improve your relationship with your child, beware that unremitting distress or troubling behaviors, yours or your child's, may need the help of professionals.

Also by Richard Bromfield

How to Turn Boys into Men without a Man around the House: A Single Mother's Guide (with Cheryl Erwin, Crown)

Playing for Real: Exploring the World of Play Therapy and the Inner Worlds of Children (Penguin USA, now available at *www.basilbooks.com*)

Teens in Therapy: Making It Their Own (W.W. Norton)

Doing Child and Adolescent Psychotherapy: Adapting Psychodynamic Treatment to Contemporary Practice (Wiley)

Handle with Care: Understanding Children and Teachers (Teachers College Press)

Get Psyched: How Your Mind Does Its Thing and What You Can Do to Help (in press, Dutton Children's Books)

About the Author

Richard Bromfield, Ph.D., is a graduate of Bowdoin College and the University of North Carolina at Chapel Hill. A faculty member of Harvard Medical School, he writes about children, psychotherapy and family life in both professional and popular periodicals. He is in private practice in both Boston and Danvers, Massachusetts.

Printed in the United States
207963BV00001B/112-114/A

9 780979 788512